People Are Puzzles

About This Book

People are Puzzles grapples masterfully with eternal themes of love, death, and identity. This debut collection features imagery-rich language complemented by interstitial sketches and paintings bursting with their own poeticism. With references spanning from flora to video games, Alastor George is a multidisciplinary creator extracting ideas both visceral and abstract.

Heady and heavy, *People are Puzzles* rewards the careful reader with unexpected metaphors and considered rhymes. Here's a book that transcends what many find restricting: conventional expectations of adolescence and the rigor of gender constructs.

—Radius Burik, Kansas City based writer, musician, editor

Responses to Individual Poems

Response to "Foxglove"
        "Drink chamomile!"
            —Bryson

Response to "Rose"

        You can't blame the Rose; it's in her nature. This poem spoke to me in more ways than one, and I think you as reader can recognize that there are many ways to look at the meaning. The poem asks you introspective questions that also challenge you to look outside of yourself, and to stop seeing in black and white (or in this case, red + white). The thorns will kill the field mouse because it's all they know to do; but that doesn't mean the thistles shouldn't be sheared away. "Boys will be boys" and "Guns will be guns."
            — Seven

People Are Puzzles

by

Alastor George

Golden Antelope Press
715 E. McPherson
Kirksville, Missouri 63501
2025

Copyright ©2025 by Alastor George
Front Cover and Interior Art by Alastor George

Cover Design by Russell Nelson

All rights reserved. No portion of this publication may be duplicated in any way without the expressed written consent of the publisher, except in the form of brief excerpts or quotations for review purposes.

ISBN   978-1-952232-96-1

Library of Congress Control Number: 2025934687

Published by:
Golden Antelope Press
715 E. McPherson
Kirksville, Missouri 63501

Available at:
Golden Antelope Press
715 E. McPherson
Kirksville, Missouri, 63501
Phone: (660) 229-2997
http://www.goldenantelope.com
Email: ndelmoni@gmail.com

Dedication

Thank you to my grandparents and parents for believing in me, and giving me the courage to explore. And thank you to those who *didn't* believe in me, for giving me the spite to go on.

Publishers' Preface

At seventeen, Alastor George is the youngest author Golden Antelope has ever published. Yet his subtlety and depth of experience are impressive. The *People Are Puzzles* front cover, which George designed, illustrates this fondness for complexity: a bonsai brain planted in a oldfashioned glass jar surrounded by eighteen small hand-written, alliterative, "p" words.* Each bit of this design is a clue about why or how people are puzzles. How is a human brain like bonsai? Why is it in a mason jar? Is cursive writing a tribute to past writers, an annoyance to present readers, or both? What's most puzzling for people who are surrounded by passion, politics, poison, progress, paradox, plastic, pathos...?** What's alliteration *for*?

For Golden Antelope, a press which does a disproportionate number of books by retired folks, Al George's work presents both challenges and delights. Some of the challenges involve technologies which we "seasoned seniors" react to the way George's peers, born in the aughts (oughts?) might be expected to react to … cursive writing, or wooden butter churns.*** Other generational challenges involve assumptions. Most "Boomers" aren't accustomed to specifying their pronouns; George's agemates joke, half in earnest, about misgenderings. We remember airports without TSA screenings; today's teens accept metal detectors in schools as normal.

Even if you are a mere quinquagenarian–in your fifties–you may feel vaguely disoriented at times as our author mixes symbols from across centuries and cultures, or assumes shared values, or experiments with poetic forms. The challenges George's work presents to readers are real. However, meeting them, considering them, is one of the core delights this book offers. People *are* puzzles, after all. The quality of the thinking, the aptness of the implied analogies, the honesty, the range of emotions processed–all are sources of delight*** as well as bridges across whatever "generation gaps" we need to cross.

And Alastor George's life has given him unusually varied experiences to process. By the time he was eight, he had lived in urban Denver and rural Kremling, CO; in Honolulu, HI, Bedford PA, Kirksville, MO, and in Wilmington, NC. His family background is eclectic. His father, who had spent several years as a missionary's child on a Navajo reservation, later worked as a musician and repaired pipelines before becoming a surveyor; his mother had studied *hijras* in India, developed a passion for gardening, worked her way up a corporate ladder, and eventually left that world to help run a used bookstore. His younger brother could identify dozens of types of dinosaurs by age four. Alastor George grew up adjusting to new accents, assumptions, and teaching methods, finding symbols in new landscapes, losing and gaining rich friendships, meeting bullies, befriending puppies, planning a career in medicine. In his teens, he came out as trans and as an advocate for "misfits" like himself.

Digging in, discovering connections, *feeling what others feel*, these are timeless, ageless traits of poets–and of healers. Alastor George has been carefully watching the world, studying its codes, symbols, and people (himself included) for seventeen rich years. In *People Are Puzzles*, he shapes symbols and questions codes as he shares human stories, especially his own.

****

* For those whose eyesight is no longer teenage-sharp, the words surrounding the *People Are Puzzles* brain-plant are: poison, passion, personal, precious, prisoner, persuasive, powerful, political, perspective, progress, pathetic, peculiar, poignant, paranoid, plastic, paradoxical, poetry, and prose.

****Consider this a trigger warning. Some of these poems will make some readers uncomfortable.**

***With the author's permission, we've inserted an occasional note. Septuagenarians can google *Kuroshitsuji*, but need help with Technoblade. More teens know *manga* than Latin.

Contents

People Are Puzzles	1
????? POETRY ?????	2
Growing Up	4
Rough Waves	5
The Shooting: A Reflection (Prose)	7
Dog Teeth	13
Awake	15
Christmas Eve	16
Goldlands	19
Names (Prose)	20
Leather and Pine	23
Symphony of Colour	25
Where Love Is (Prose)	26
14 February, 2023	27
Soldier in Pink	28
Orange	29
You Probably	30
FarFar Away	32
Ribs	34
Lotus Flower	37
Aurum Mendaciolum	38
Foxglove and Arsenic	39
Foxglove	40
Respite	46
Glass	47

Lust For Illusions	48
Good Morning	49
Relapse: Reprise	50
Searching for One's Self	51
Lady in Gold	54
Snowblind	55
For Them	57
Don My Armour	59
Covered by Your Grace	61
Anger Born of Worry	62
Western Roads: Colorado	63
Bleeding-Heart Dove	68
Better In Blue	70
Rose	72
Sunflower	74
Romanticise	76
The Little Things	78
Feeling of Mine	79
Dandelions	80
CNN: The World's Ending (Again)	81

People Are Puzzles

????? POETRY ?????

I never quite understood poetry
Melancholy, happy, angry with empathy
A boundless playground *in theory*
Yet there's still a standard to read / reach

A certain threshold of quality
In an art of no measure
You can rhyme or not
You can keep a rhythm unless you don't want to then just don't
slang? Sure m8

The goal is to make someone *feel*
Release chemistry in their cerebrums
Be relatable, appear real
Create impressions that you *see* them

Weave a tale, true or false
Establish a pattern or not
Make it easy to digest
But make them feel smart
Publishers like cash
You like making art

You start writing for a reason
Tell a story, vent a feeling

But when you send that first manuscript,
Type up that first doc
The threat of corporatism ...
Part of you gets stuck

And when your whole point
Is up for interpretation
And the industry standard

Is to be different from corporation's–
Publishing and writing
Can be really frickin' hard.

I can't ask my readers
"Do you get the metaphor?"
I can't reach through the page to ask
"Wanna know the lore?"
It's difficult to find a gift
when you don't know who it's for.

Sometimes I think back
To Ms. B's English class
When I got an A
By googling "what rhymes with apple"
And everything felt so easy.

Growing Up

As months and years pass
People seem to change
Ironically things shifting
Is all that stays the same

The only constant is turning
The hands ticking on a clock
The sands of time move on
Never slowing, never to stop.

As your surroundings change
So does your mentality
Those whom you idolize
Their bodies, personalities.

A decade or so ago
Taylor Swift was my go-to
Then Harriet Tubman, Misty Copeland
Somebody new

I can find solace in myself now
Though I will still look elsewhere
I don't so often wish to *be* them
I'm not content, but self-aware.

Rough Waves

Far out deep
In the North Sea
An oil rig stands
Solitary

Abandoned and alone
With rough waves lapping
Support beams cracking
Spurdogs passing

While down in the depths
You can't hear the roar
The water is calm
Smooth to the floor

The crashing waves and tempest
That all but Vikings feared
Beneath the rough waves
Simply disappear

The water on the surface
Swells fluctuating
But at the blue's prettiest
It's simply suffocating.

And those born in tempest
Often seek it out
Return to their brood
Despite the brooding clouds

The calm feels foreign
Warmth, a strange embrace
Whilst turbulence provides
A more familiar face

To be wild and free
May be comforting
Some find it preferable
To be lost at sea

One may yearn for the currents
That might leave one drowned
If whirlpools be comparable
To where one was housed

Adrift on the waves
Though capsizing may occur
It's easier to suffer through
To leave things as they were

Unwise waters
To sail, yet still
Rough waves give
A homely sort of thrill

For homes that were a tempest
Unpredictable ports
Often give way
To unpredictable sorts

The oil rig stands
Longing for beneath
To see deep life pass by
Never realising

Underwater it would rust
Nevermind drown
Rough waves are cold
But there's a reason they're around

The Shooting: A Reflection

The shooting.

Soon it shall be lost to New Hanover High, reduced only to retellings and rumours. I am a senior, and it was my freshman year. Once my class graduates, it will follow with us, and the freshman of 2025-2026 will never know the stories of the students that day.

There is no monument on the front steps, there were no vigils held over the week following. All we got was one day off of school, and a complimentary announcement saying you should go talk to your councillor if you can't stop thinking about the gunshots resounding throughout the courtyard.

The shooting wasn't one of those shootings that the nation heard about, it wasn't one that tik tok edits were made over, it wasn't one that had solemn newscasters passing tissues to sobbing teachers mid-inter-view. It was not a "never again" shooting; it was the sort that the sophomores tell the rising freshman about in study hall, or the juniors talk about in groups, going over their personal experiences over and over, memorising every detail of that day. They share every step from the moment they got off the bus, to the moment they were escorted to the Williston gym by cops with big guns and picked up by worried parents.

And then they discuss the response from the school board. How the superintendent wore Gucci shoes the next day. How Ms. Hash played a movie that opened with a gunshot sound.

Author's note: as I was typing this, we went into lockdown.

That's a thing about New Hanover (so far). We've

only had one actual shooting, but we've had countless swattings, lockdowns, guns on campus, and fights that get out of hand. I remember in my sophomore year we had a lockdown every day for eight school days in a row.

That's a crazy thing to say, we *only* had *one* actual shooting, that's something I've heard over and over, like it somehow invalidates what everyone went through that day. That's like if someone hits you with their car and the nurse at the hospital says "well, at the Smithfield hospital, someone was hit by a *bus*" and expects that sentence to heal the injuries you sustained.

We weren't a "never again" shooting. We were a shooting that was kept to the local news, a shooting at a low income school that the county did not care about, nevermind the nation. We were a shooting that had students trading different video angles like playing cards.

I did that for a while too, I've since deleted all but one of the recordings, I don't need them, I've committed them to memory.

Part of me needs to remember– the orange of the catwalk walls, the paw prints that are still painted on the floor, how the video cuts off before you see the blood spill over the wildcat's tracks. You can hear the gunshots and see the crowd disperse.

They run away any way they can, scattering like that scene in *Ratatouille* where they're all running to the walls. The video cuts off before you hear the screams, before you can pick out the terrified few who stood still, frozen by fear. The video cuts off before you see the upperclassmen compose themselves, dragging those petrified kids by their wrists towards the parking lot.

I was in 3rd block by that point, my friend Whitely hadn't gotten there yet, she was supposed to be in class with me, she wasn't; she was with my other friend Bailey, piling as many students as they could fit into their hand-me-down cars and driving as far and fast away as their engines would take them. My friend Brooklyn was supposed to be in AP Psych, but she was running a bit late. She ended up trampled by the crowd, scraping her arm against the cinderblock as the horde of children clawed desperately through each other to the exit. She still has a scar from where the rough bricks chafed off her skin in strips.

I wasn't heroic, guiding scared freshmen to the gas station down the road, or Folks Cafe' across the street. I was a freshman, in the basement with my theatre teacher, a yellow plush blanket wrapped around my shoulders.

And after hours of waiting in the dark, literally and figuratively, we heard bangs resounding from above us. Something about the basement of New Hanover High: there's a door in the tech booth that connects to the girls' locker room that the wrestling club uses. Sometimes Ms. Harding would have to bang on the door to get them to pipe down during rehearsals.

We weren't used to banging coming from the other side of the door though....

I'll always remember that banging. I'll always remember the way they pointed their flashlights at us, the light obscuring the faces behind them and boring into my pupils, telling us to put our hands up and get on our knees.

I'll always remember how my blanket dropped from my shoulders as I raised my palms to the musty, asbestos-filled ceiling.

I'll always remember the feeling of the cold, metal gun poking my back, making contact through my shirt. It wasn't personal, just police policy.

They told us to gather our stuff quickly, which was difficult for me. I had to stuff my blanket back into my bag as we were being ushered out the door by a SWAT team.

Cause we weren't a "never again" shooting, we weren't a "never forget" shooting. So I *need* to remember. Because who else will?

My boyfriend heard about the shooting before the first students were formally evacuated. He was calling, and texting, messaging me on Discord and text, calling me, calling my *mom*. They both knew what was happening, but nothing about it; all they knew was that I wasn't picking up my phone.

Another thing about the basement, there's no cell service, you need to go to the top of the stairs to get a single bar. My theory is that the lead in the walls blocks your signal.

I'll always remember the next day we went to school, we got a singular day off to collect ourselves and be ready to work again. The nice teachers gave us a week of movies and colouring pages. Ms. Kerr was really nice, she gave us plenty of time, she didn't start teaching again until she made sure everyone was ready. Other teachers told us to shove it down and got straight back to classwork.

Sometimes I'll hear younger students ask why the seniors always talk about the shooting anytime something happens, they say we're making it a "personality trait." I think we love talking about it, because we've been told not to.

Because we were shoved right back into the routine before we had a chance to process it. And the freshman will never truly understand why the seniors jump every time the intercom buzzes. The conversations with students are the only chance we *get* to talk about it. To process it in the little way we can.

My sophomore year, students went missing. One turned up dead. I feel like I shouldn't put her name in here, I feel like I don't have the right.

We talked once, I'll always remember it, we talked about ramen. It was brief, but she was so sweet. No one knew what happened to her for about a week. Turns out her brother killed her. I'll always remember what he did to her body.

And I'll always remember the front of the school. Covered in red, red roses, red presents, all surrounding the picture of her in her red shirt. I made a red rose out of paper in French class. I did it instead of the assignment but JROD (my teacher) didn't mind. He knew who it was for.

Our school's colours are black and orange, you'd think that red would go with it. It doesn't, it stands out against the century old brick. Too different to match, too similar to contrast.

When she turned up, butchered by her own blood, in a pool of her own blood, the school said "you should go talk to your councillor if you miss her too much to focus in class." Over the intercom, the buzz made all of the juniors and seniors jump reflexively.

I wonder if red was still her favourite colour till the end.

And I've always felt like I don't have the right to grieve. Because I only knew her smile in passing, because I wasn't one of the brave students on the catwalk when those gunshots went off, because somewhere in the world, there's someone who got hit by a bus, instead of a car.

But I need to; if I don't, who will? When the school shoves you back into class after one day off, when you get significantly better at cardio because of all the running away you need to do to survive – in a place that's supposed to be safe– one needs to remember. **I know** that when a tree falls in the forest it *does* make a sound, and that even if there are no humans around to hear it, the ecosystem will still be affected. The birds will remember, the squirrels will remember, the mycelium and saplings will remember, the elk that eats its leaves will remember, and the wildcat that eats that elk will notice.

But when the nation forgets, who will remember?

Sadly, that falls on the shoulders of the students.

The students who can't forget.

The students who can't vote yet, to decide the legislature.

Old enough to die for it, but too young to have a voice about it.

And old enough to be forgotten. Common enough that there are schools, where no one says "never again." They say "oh, it happened again. " Again and again and again

Again and again, nobody says "never again."

DOG TEETH

My claws came out today
In a sick and frightened way
What I've been trained to do
Show a hostile display.

I have the teeth of a dog
A savage old maw
Sharp are my canines
Weary is my jaw

I've slowly grown accustomed
To the taste of blood
To the taste of bitters
To the sting of loss

And though they've grown dull
From years of disuse
My instinct remains
To snap my teeth at you.

I can't get away
From what I was trained to say
It's the expense of defence
The quips and cracks I've made

Silver is my tongue
Though the air burns my lungs
Cause I was taught to punch
How many times I'll lunge

Some days I will revel
Teeth yellowed with plaque
My heart beats loud
When yours starts to crack

Some days I regret
Feel shame without remorse
Manufacture my own guilt
Cause I can't feel yours

Cause I grew up with Goliath
But no stones to throw or sling
I spent my days from 3 years old
Watching him in the ring

And I grew up South of Eden
Far away from Mecca
I was reared for 16 years
On an unholy vendetta

I have dog teeth
And an indecisive heart
But tragedy is in my blood
And pain's what I impart

AWAKE

The scent of booze so heavy on his breath
I can taste it in my nostrils
Smell it in the mist

Wine redder than blood
Stronger than beer
Alcohol and cigarettes
Or razors so near

Every night we'd spill red
Be that wine or blood
A razor or a mug

Sleep escaping my grasp
As I settle for a fake
Staying "clean"
Whatever that means
Just to feel awake

CHRISTMAS EVE

A dreary night
A candle alight
I've come to find
A wish for less life

One borne without contempt
Not entropy, more apathy
Yet the die was rolled
And life was chose

With such blood in my veins
We could call it luck
Or lack thereof

Shall I try?
conceptualise?
Shall I attempt? Only to fail,
Via cowardice or incompetence,
What can only be described
As a hypothetical suicide?

Above, bright, so far apart
The twinkling of lonely stars
From so far away, they look connected
But each alone feels neglected

Floating alone in the dark void of space
Gravity pulling at a glacial pace
And by the time the stars meet and collide
Life on earth will have long since died

The candle light shines
But blisters on my skin
Leaving alabaster white
With a stinging red stain

Outside there's a canvas, a world of white
The hollowness of a sombre night
Footprints fade into the snow
Like in memories I used to know

Sledding down the yard
To the neighbours' old tree
Hanging ornaments
Walking to the creek

Every gift so simple
Every smile so bright
Christmas dinner so happy
With warmth in every bite

So fond am I of memories
Naught but an echo inside me
I can only hope in the winter mist
That someone out there *knows how to live*

I don't yearn for death
But renewal of a life
Which now seems so stale
Through the marching of time

I'm not in pursuit
of a way to die
I've just been looking for a place
Where my spirit's still alive

And in such a bitter quest
I've endangered that last part
Stewing in what could've been
Has festered my red heart

GOLDLANDS

    One day I'll find the goldlands
    A part of me called home
    Home is where the heart is
    But mine's grown sad and cold
    Home for me was company
    Now I'm all alone
    The bleeding organ beats *resent*
    Where once it held my hope

    One day I'll find the goldlands
    A part of me called home
    Where silver streams bend
    Beside the twisted oak
    Where water runs warm
    And paper boats once flowed
    Now they've all but sunk
    Yet they're part of what we're owed
    One day I hope to find them
    In a place we once called home.

NAMES

My junior year, my English III teacher had the whole class write a few pages on what our names meant to us.

I had the unique liberty of choosing my own name. My old name was many things, it was beautiful, it meant "beautiful". But it was not me.

I started my transition when I was around 12, and the name situation took a while to sort out. To this day I still have a 2 page list in the notes app on my phone, two pages of potential names.

I chose Alastor. The first letter was the same as my old name, so I could sign everything "A. George."

"Alastor" felt strong and stoic, the looping A's and O's took up space. It was a name that you could stamp onto a piece of paper and it would say "I am here," tone brooking no argument.

In other words, everything I wanted to be.

There are two main origins of the name, Celtic and Greek. Despite the fact that my family is majorly Celtic, I chose the Greek name.

Αλάστωρ, phoneticised to Alastor, was an epithet of Zeus. It means either "Destroyer" or "Protector of man" depending which side of the battlefield you're on. Boiled down, it means "Avenger"

I am very proud of my Celtic heritage, but the Celtic spelling was too dainty for me. "Allister" had too many thin strokes. Undeniably a good name, but not for me.

Even though I am quite thin, and my grandma would argue that I am beautiful, that is not the point of a name.

A name does not describe the body we inhabit, rather it addresses the humanity inside, be that a trait we wish upon our children (EX: Sofia, meaning "wise") or a reference to history, the past that built our present, as we will build the future (EX: Jameson, meaning "son of james").

My name to me is the power to build my own future, to redefine who I am to the people around me.

When I changed my name, I lost a lot of friends, It didn't help that COVID struck not a month after. So I was stuck at home, and half the people I'd trusted for the whole of middle school now refused to talk to me.

So when I came to New Hanover High School, I did so with a chip on my shoulder, I was expecting confrontation and so I prepared myself by being cold and mean. I stamped my name as hard as I could at the top of every assignment. As if to say "Look, I am here. D'ya have a problem with that?"

Thankfully the people at NHHS met my hostility with confusion, they were patient and kind to this scrawny kid in a suit, with ice in his eyes. Their body language saying "what the heck dude, chill out."

By the end of the first quarter, I'd learned the difference between being mean, and being firm. The Queer and Allied role models I met showed me that it's okay to be okay, that I could express happiness without making myself vulnerable. Thankfully, after COVID, I warmed back up to normal socialisation quickly.

I was able to do so because people saw me, not as the name on their roster, "beauty," or as the body that walked through the halls. But as me, the humanity inside of me.

I could grow, to be strong enough to protect the younger queer kids, the rising freshman, walking through the halls with ice in their eyes and grit in their teeth. To show them that its okay to be okay, and you don't have to expect attacks, even in the South. I could be strong, but for them.

Everything I wanted to be, and was.

LEATHER AND PINE

For my friend, Pinetree

I'm gagging on the ashes
From the fire we once were
But I alone could not fuel us
The spark faded to a blur

The embers slowly dying
Choking on your pine
Borders somehow quelled
What only lightning could ignite

Smoke fills my lungs
And I try to reach out
But I stirrup the coal dust
So I try another route

I try to call out,
Past the roar of the wind
See through the texan sun
My eyes red rimmed

You're already gone
The dust smothered the flames
I sit and I wonder
Who is to blame

Your parents for dragging
You all the way out here
Just to get you
Away from us queers?

Me for not trying
Ever hard enough?
It's hard to make contact
When phone lines are cut

I'm gagging on the ashes
From the fire we once were
But alone, I could not fuel us
The spark faded to a blur

The embers slowly dying
Choking on your pine
Borders somehow quelled
What only lightning could ignite

SYMPHONY OF COLOUR

Their voice echoes yellow

Though first it comes out green

Somewhere along the lines it's grey

Before it shifts to pink

They fade into sapphiric blue

Rippling royal purple

Then green's renewed...

A nebula of senses
A galaxy of taste

Your colours flow,
invisible to most,
but vibrant in my brain.

WHERE LOVE IS

Love is in the small things.

I could tell from the scent that he had washed his hair this morning, I could tell by the taste that he'd put on chapstick while I was in the bathroom. Because *he* could tell that I needed to go soon and our goodbye kiss was coming up.

I could tell that he'd stopped using the Burts Bees chapstick his mother got him and started using the fruit one *he* likes.

Even if we don't see each other in person for a month, we start back up right where we left off, only acknowledging that time passed in the brief moment where we exchange the backlog of gifts.

I'm not good at expressing love. Sometimes I would wonder if I was aromantic, just because I forgot how to let myself feel the emotion.

I forgot, not love itself, but where love is.

Love is in the small, pure, beautiful things.

14 FEBRUARY, 2023

Like bile without the burn
A sheep without his herd
Like glass without the stain
Window without a pane

Peas without the pod
Like berries on a stalk
A canvas without paint
A thought without a brain

Whoever knew
That today without you
Is Valentine's dismay–
Just February's cold day

SOLDIER IN PINK*

For Alexander / Technoblade (June 1, 1999-June, 2022)

When so came the cursed day
In June when the stars began to fray,
In the night when your soul chose to fly away,
When Valhalla opened its oaken archway

For you, the soldier clad in pink,
1,000 blades were raised in sync;
Even Odin raises his drink
For the soldier clad in pink

Silver armour tinted in red
Certain armour that caused so much dread
Stolen crown of a king long dead
by the soldier whose name's unsaid

When so comes the cursed day
In June, through that open oaken archway
What would've been another birthday
Is now my fond soldier's death anniversary.

*An iconic figure in the world of Youtube and Minecraft, the genius known as Technoblade died just after turning 23; millions of fans mourned and paid tribute with messaging, art, graffiti, gaming, and donations for cancer research.

ORANGE

(For Bruegel's Icarus Falling; *For Toby Fox's* Undertale)

>Green lights float ahead
>The cliff and the sword
>Who dreams when you're dead?
>
>Orange petals fallen down
>With a body on the ground
>Like buttercups did once
>
>At the age of fifteen
>Complex fulfilled
>Just freshly released
>Now he lay, killed.

YOU PROBABLY

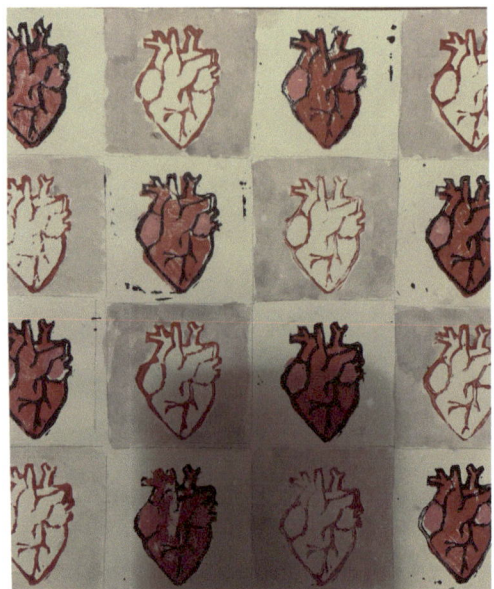

You probably think I'm awful don't you?
Through offset pages in signatures of eight*
Through the harrowing cynicism and obvious hate
Through blood money, and blood of mine
Each slice crossing yet another line
Your thoughts on me appear to be true

Just another layer to cut through
Through Styrofoam-dermis and fat
Blood dripping in splatters and taps
Bubbling yellow and down near the bone
Through muscular systems and nerves disowned
Pretending I can't feel the tissue

I promise you none of my screws are loose
Digging up my own grave is entirely sane
In an effort to feel at home again
Sabotaging my only hope of rest;
Chaos, entropy, it's what I do best
All I need now is to push through

Can we sit in the yard like we used to?
Averse to all change
Pretending we're the same
Ignoring that you're gone
Clover crowns and bon-bons
You really think I'm awful, don't you?

*Offset presses print in multiples (signatures) of eight, sixteen, or thirty-two pages at a time. Signatures of eight tend to be used in specialized small books, zines, or journals.

FARFAR AWAY*

The head of the table is empty
For grandfather dearest has passed
Our Farfar so far away
Time passes too slow yet too fast

The table is still set and neat
And manners are still left intact
Yet elbows keep hitting the table
Each time we feel the lack

Only air sits in the chair
Eyes trace the empty space
There's a moment's hesitation
As we decide who will say grace.

It feels so incredibly backwards
To sit in the library alone
And think of the story of Moses
The bible pulled up on my phone

I try to recall all the details
But King James doesn't tell it quite right
Maybe it's not the inflection
Maybe the screen's just too bright

The Tyndale says it too bluntly
The story still hangs in the air
It hovers just out of reach
Close enough I can tell that it's there.

The night is ending so quiet
As though the home's just a house;
Despite the cream-coloured carpet
I'm sure I could hear any mouse

Eventually everything's over
Dinner's dishes finally clean
And from the space between the lines
I see what could've been

The things I'd planned to say
All but melt away
Washed off by tidal waves
Like the sauce from dinner's plates

Like memories knocked off the mantle
Photographs covered or moved
The jar of lollipops gone
Lost or shoved out of view

The night   slowly   passes
Breakfast comes as planned
I eat the off-brand cereal
Though it tastes exceedingly bland

The head of the table is empty
For grandfather dearest is dead
And my lovely grieving grandmother
Can't stand to sit at the other end.

*"Farfar" is the Swedish word for "Grandfather." Our Farfar was a science teacher, a Methodist minister, and a wrestling coach.

RIBS

for Daisy, (June 15, 2024)

I'll feel forever guilty
For cutting your life short
Though it'd been agonising
Mere days of naught but hurt

I hadn't seen your ribs
Since the day we got you
And I witness them again
The day I held and lost you

For the first time in a decade
They were poking through your skin
Your skin which is still warm
Which has grown paper thin

Your skin that had been scarred
And it makes me reel
That in that cherished decade
Those scars had slowly healed

Your skin is getting cold
Your heart has fully stopped
And though it's losing warmth
Your fur is still so soft

You have been my favourite
Since I was merely six
Since the day we picked you
We were two misfits

You had scars on you
And I had them in me
And through each other's moments
We'd be there, guaranteed

I hadn't seen your ribs
Since the time our bond was born
But now you finally relax
And I see them in your form

I think the worst part
Was *knowing* you were gone
When the crematorium asked
If they should print your paws

They took you away
Or rather took your body
I went outside later
And the sky'd gone foggy

It had rained that day
It was not forecasted
But dew littered the leaves
The earth mourned your passing.

And I can feel *my* ribs
I didn't eat all day
And now that it's night
My room's in disarray

Hadn't had time to clean
Because you were so sick
I didn't want to lose time
It wasn't worth the risk

I press a pillow to my chest
And hope to feel the warmth
That cuddling with you brought me
Before your fur went cold

Press and squeeze so very close
But never close enough
Acutely feel the lack of you
The feeling just too **ruff**

No matter now how hard I press
Its only just a pillow
It will not fill the hole
I don't want to let you go

My chest feels stuffed with cotton
All around my ribs
But the actual cavity
Is where my heart has been

It's nauseatingly hollow now
I feel naught but the lack
What my ribs had sworn to protect
Crumbled and turned black.

LOTUS FLOWER

With a nod to Homer's Odyssey

You, my friend, drip
Syrupy sweet
From truthless petals
I shall not receive

You, my love, live
The purest fallacy
Euphoric like a drug
A pattern of deceit

You, my friend, die
Brown once pink and green
Leaving those you touch
In a factoid of agony

AURUM MENDACIOLUM

"Golden Little Lies"

Upon a throne of gilded lies I sit
As the world around me burns
Gilded not golden
Merely the illusion of grandeur
Ash floating in the air
Like powdered sugar or snow
A burning cold as though ice and salt
Simultaneously graced my tongue

You drove us to this fate
With the insistence that
You. Were. Right.
Going to the ends of the earth
To prove your little lies

So here I sit
Atop a throne of them all
Sorting through the rubbage and wreckage
Trying to find the truth.

And perhaps if you say it enough times
The salt will be that of caviar
The bitter taste in my mouth actually fine espresso
And the ash will transform into flurries.

But until then
I'll keep searching
Within the gilded lies.

FOXGLOVE AND ARSENIC

"Foxglove and Arsenic" was the first of several poems using the poisonous flower foxglove to talk about this person (who will remain anonymous). Written nearly 4 years ago, those 4 years have been years of upheaval and evolution in my friendship with them.

You're foxglove, I'm arsenic
Equally toxic
My lab, your garden
Burning teapot, brass arsonist

I'm the maker of angels
Brass wings disdainful
Sprouted feathers painful
I'm your anthrax in the mail

You're a flower brewed in tea
Pink petals, black debris
Oleander guarantee
But without the dignity

I'm arsenic, you're foxglove
Your farm club, my brass gun
And through all the toxin
Shines the lie of your "love"

I feel as though this unedited original, though not up to the standard I hold myself to now, is important for understanding the long poem that follows.

FOXGLOVE

I can't stand the taste
Of Foxglove in my tea
When arsenic carries
Much more dignity

And I can't stand the look
Of the petals white and pink
Or the taste of toxin
Floating in my drink

The specks pass, black
Pieces of debris
Unappetizing sheen
Oleander guarantee

For much like a lotus
Or an oleander tree
You'd perish if I leave
Or so you keep telling me…

You're Apocynaceae
Apocalyptic spring
Your flowers burst forth
Swarming, smothering

And every single time
We'd fight or disagree
I'd be your arsenic
Your poison of the week

You'd call me up that night
To cut the deadly bryony
Swearing it's the end
And I'd call the police

Your threats don't bounce
At least off of me
You're the reason there are bars
On the Jubilee.

Even columbine's pretty
The flower one, I mean
But that too has its deadly
Cardio-genic properties

And you make my heart stop
Every time I see
Your face or your name
Or your caller ID

You've called me hemlock
The maker of angels
Just call me arsenic
Since I'm so blame-able.

To look innocent
From exterior angles
You play the victim,
Make yourself breakable

I can't stand
Remaining ever faithful
To a flower so pretty
Yet so deeply fatal

You've dug your way in
Your vines so baneful
Under my skin
It's unbearable

Still I keep fighting
To keep you stable
Yet some plants wither
And we're simply unable…

I dedicated myself
But was met with betrayal
With lies and flies
And stinking uranyl *

Your toxin-tipped kisses
Were clouding my head
Too much to see
That this had to end

Wisteria's invasive
Its vines choke and spread
But people think it's pretty
It is, granted…

Nothing's wholly bad
Even dwale and lead
But we cannot ignore
The negative effects

Datura is lovely
But we cannot pretend….
Antifreeze may taste sweet
Doesn't mean that it's your friend

And foxglove is pretty
But its beauty is a lie
One steeps in such a flower
And surely they may die

End up another skeleton
Rotted by the blight
That's syphoning the soul
Of roots nearby

*Uranyl is a toxic oxycation of uranium.

The scars on your wrists
Match those on my hands
As I offer my skin
To meet your demands

Throw me to the side
Like your other dogs
When it's inconvenient
To feed me, Pavlov

But your benefit's unceasing;
Receive, then have me shot.
You thrive while I die,
Get everything you want

And despite this fortune
Your never-ending luck
You cry to those around you
To give everything we've got

And we huddle in
As you throw your bombs
Screaming you're the victim
And begging we respond

That we leave our safety
Abandon our walls
To bring you lies of comfort
While you sob it's not your fault

You're waited on
Hand and foot
Your toddler-tantrums
Overlooked

I hope the other
Shoe will drop
I hope one day
You'll be caught

I hope for your
Tragic demise
For you to burn
Among your lies.

But though it hurts
To god above
I pray that you'll
Find peace and love

That somewhere in
That turbulent soul
You'll find someone
Who can make you whole

So you can stop
Sucking dry
All those who
Enter your life

And I don't even
Believe in god
(Maybe some social
Part of me does…)

And I hate that you're wonderful
And beautiful and sweet
I hate that I feel compelled
To give every part of me

Every last drop
Of nectar in my soul
Of iron in my blood
To the oleander toll

I hate that I once thought
That I was arsenic
That arsenic could stand
Against your gardening

I hate that petals push
And flowers overpower
Chemical reactions
Within our very atoms

And I hate the taste
Of foxglove in my tea
But I'll be damned, where I stand
Foxglove's gotten me.

RESPITE

Rest unto those who can't rest on their own
Solace to those who've lost all their hope

A minute of respite to those who can't sleep
A second to give you a chance to breathe

A shoulder to cry on
A pat on the head
A drop of affection
When they forget who I am

A minute to pretend that I'm someone better
A hug, a listen, a gift, a letter

I'll be your replacement for just a day
I can take all that weight away

I can become who you want me to be
I just wish that sometimes, you'd want me to be *me.*

GLASS

Water down my hands
Wash off the red
Water down my throat
Clean out my head
My water's full of glass
Out of shock, I dropped the cup
Now there's water and glass
And it's all mixed up
Now I can't quite tell
What's real, what's not.

LUST FOR ILLUSIONS

I want to hold on
To that feeling
To false control.
To the power of deception
The deception of power
The elation of believing
I am god.

I want to hold on
To that euphoric high
Higher in the sky
Than any drug can take me
Or any cut provide
To adrenaline and honest happiness

I want to hold on
To the inconsequential anger
The throat of delusion
The grandeur that held me by my ego
And kept me afloat
By making me believe
That I was truly invulnerable

I want to hold on to that
But I can't.

GOOD MORNING

To the sick bastard I wake up and see:
In the morning when linoleum graces my feet
Emanating exhaustive apathy
Twisting into a fallacy
That lie you tell, time after time
Your green eyes reversely mimicking mine

To the obnoxious prick I meet with after lunch:
What I wouldn't pay to watch you get punched
To see that mirthless, smug grin knocked off your face
To see bruises and blood put you in your place

Sense of empathy
Long since abandoned
Replaced by apathy and anarchy
In tandem.

It's clear it hurts you
To say it again and again
The bitter taste
Of your verbal defence

Those cringey little moments
When you say something wrong
When you mess up the story
And the veil's all gone

To the monster I see in the night:
To the regrets that haunt your life
To that ever-lasting guilt that couldn't be clearer
I bid thee adieu, devil in the mirror

RELAPSE: REPRISE

No career is linear

Every rhythm has its rests

Relapse makes you no inferior

The steps back are part of the dance

SEARCHING FOR ONE'S SELF*

I was lucky enough to be born into money
But raised with vinegar, not festering honey
Brought up with a lack of false piety
Expecting only a void awaiting me

When the faerie lights fade
And so ends another day
I am left in my living room
Assuming my new place

When the rainbows leave the shelves
I start searching for myself
Searching how to deal
Remembering how I've dealt

I know I'm not that great
But something needs to change
I want more than just a name
Written on my grave

***

Markets crashed in twenty-eleven
I came into the world in two thousand seven
Born in god's country, without hope of heaven
Lethargically searching for eager expression...

I've mingled with swells and paupers
I've rebelled against teachers and fathers
Despite watchers and blockers and mockers
I know that I'll be my own author

Life is not without its struggles
And sometimes I'm forced to buckle
Under these sisyphean puzzles
Under the weight of pointless troubles.

But respite can be found
And I want to make a sound
Create something profound
Before I end up in the ground

Forever slow-dancing alone
In the discomfort of my own home–
Is this cursed fluorescent light
All I'll ever know?

***

Perhaps I'll break the illusion
Perhaps I'll find some solution
Maybe with tears next year
I'll finally feel effusive

Perhaps next Pride
Won't end with July
We'll be recognised
We won't need to hide

I am left longing for a season that can't be obtained
Yearning for a year without the constraints
Aching for my community again
For my queer umbrella to block out the rain

***

Wishful thinking
Won't ease the loneliness
When those who understand me
Fade into the abyss

Acclimating to the
"Normal way of life"
Which I can't get ahold of
No matter how hard I try

I am but one among many
Continuation of monotony
Society and I
That is our dichotomy

It's exhausting
Always taunting
A new box every month...
It's daunting

Constantly shifting
To find what's missing
When support is revoked
I'm viewed as twisted

***

Society and I
Building castles in the sky
Only to be torn down
At the end of Pride

Fragments in my mind
A broken mirror's all I find
Pieces of an identity
Labels I've assigned

I understand my body
I say my mind too
I dream that someday
The latter may be true

Society and I
Just to stay alive
I cater to their whims
That's my sacrifice.

*This poem was previously published in the North Carolina Bards Poetry Anthology.

LADY IN GOLD

Lady in gold
Who will speak of your sorrows
When all the world sees
Is the shine of your skin?

Lady in gold
What will come of tomorrow
When I know in hindsight
Through what you've been.

You were made a prop
Yet hardly rewarded
Not to occupy thought
But to sit on velvet

You're a sycophant on satin
Silk hides what's within
Servant to the famous
Gold hides the bruises on your skin

Did you ever speak up?
I haven't the courage to check
Did we ever sit together
Twin bruises on our necks

SNOWBLIND

Breathing till my lungs ache
In till my ribs crack
It's been years since we spoke
Nine to be exact

Yet your burning chemical kisses
Breathed by sandpaper tongue
Your eyes tracing my body
The fantasies you've spun

Blinded by the shine
Of your burning chemical kiss
All I can see is white
You linger in the mist

The idea that you could fester
Something so dear to me
That you could taint beauty itself
Is simply sickening

And fallen far from Eden
Your canines glitter, Cain,
And I am barely Able
To stand hearing that name

"Beauty"* in blonde
Like light like the sun
Like snowblinded kids
And sandpaper tongues

"Beauty" in youth
When beauty is dead
A name I abandoned
A name god himself condemned

Hearing it stops my heart
Rings hollow in my chest
My chest that aches with air
My chest that i repress

It feels all too human
Too grounded in the flesh
I desperately disconnect
For nine years… to be exact.

*"Beauty" is a translation of a long-popular female name.

FOR THEM

Everything about me
Is for somebody else
Someone who won't exist
Someone who's never felt

Who will never feel
Who will never know
The destruction they've brought
Or the lengths to which I'll go

To undo the damage
Of their disgusting thought
The idea of their existence…
It makes me distraught

For this awful creature
Not even a human soul
This revolting clump of cells
Would have utmost control

And thank the lord below
That they'll never occur
That they'll remain a conception
An *idea* of a saboteur

And curse the lord above
For imagining the thought
For conceiving the idea
Of conception and its rot.

For everything about me
Is for somebody else
My chest, my hips, my legs
My organs to my breast

All that I despise
About this cursed shell
From the day of my birth
Was to birth someone else

Every month I bleed
Every night I heal
By dreaming it's corrected...
Then I wake up to the real

All my grief
In my dysphoria
Is for the mere idea
Of infusoria*

All this rage
And effort, pain, and drought
Is for the child
I pray to live without.

*Infusoria traditionally refered to single-cell organisms swimming in decaying organic matter.

DON MY ARMOUR

Today I don my armour
Like I did the day before
Repetitive preparation
For the new day's war

First I don my breastplate
Block attacks before they start
Hope no one will question
When they see what I haven't got

Next I don my chain
Tunic high of collar
Tag of "Ralph Lauren"
Cotton shielding honour

Next I pick my flag
My banner and my colour
Tied tight as a noose
Serving silken cover

Next I don the set
My pants will match my jacket
Overdress, overcompensate
Don't get labeled as a faggot

My armour serves me well
Though I feel like a spy
What you call going stealth
Behind enemy lines

I'll disguise my voice
Though the air stings my lungs
My throat starts to croak
And my tongue weighs a ton

I'll don my socks and shoes
Black Oxfords that click
Shined, laced, no brogues
Run away from conflicts

I will wear my war paint
And hope that with a glower
You won't question my manhood
If I exude enough power

Maybe if I take up space
And keep my head held high
Slick my hair back
You mightn't dare question…maybe I…

Traditionally masculine
Tight-laced stern and cold
Maybe if I wear a suit
You'll believe what you're told

I can hope that you'll assume
That I am just clean shaven
Less androgynous I dress
Less room for interpretation

Because the biggest thing I fear
Within this mortal world
Is that you'll take a look at me
And think that I'm a girl.

COVERED BY YOUR GRACE

Covered by your grace
I stand
An unholy creation
In an unholy land
Predispositioned
To the life you impart
In this vessel of sin
Damned to fall apart

ANGER BORN OF WORRY

As dear Shakespeare said
"A rose by any other name would smell as sweet"

likewise, anger born of worry is just as unmeet

You had my heart in mind
When you unleashed your wrath

But that does not take the sting
Away from the slap

I understand the instinct
To snap when you're scared

I understand the instinct
To protect when you care

I understand the instinct
But you're making things worse

Your attempt at assistance
Results in mutual hurt.

WESTERN ROADS: COLORADO

The trees bend and twist
on windswept dry plains

coated in the golden
of grass and wild grains

that sway in the light
catching the sun's rays

illuminating stalks
a maze of veins of maize

a land so untouched
by waste and hurricanes

so unlike my new home
yet such familiar terrain

drive past pastures
horses and their manes

those will glitter too
though more a varied shade

trails so old
for such a young place

rocks cannot compare
to Appalachia's withered face

the land so organic
seems geometric from a plane

the view made of squares
farms of man-made shapes

roads are lined by towns
small but unconstrained

with shockingly fresh sushi
for a landlocked state

though you can still feel
the scorching and the flames

though healed outwardly
some trees still blackened, stained

and you can spot the markers
of shallow, hasty graves

their makers gone to Oregon
trails trailed by remains

those who made the journey
before the likes of trains

by their covered wagons
oxen bore the strain

and then there are the natives
and their lost refrains

forced out of their homes
and falsely promised aid

the mountains may be young
comparing geo-age

but to us tiny humans
and our tiny human brains…

the sand dunes got there
from lost ancient waves

the valley was an ocean
far before our age

and now it's bone dry
scorched by seasoned flames

we can't have fireworks
even on holidays

and the air is thin
up in the raised

still cut by coyotes
and their nightly wails

the deer are in velvet
March's shed misplaced

to be found in the woods
for the wild is more tame

than is any city
or concrete maze

mountain mist falls
in thick morning veils

personal mist falls
with every exhale

snow in June
the mountain retains

for even in summer
it's cold in the raised.

Up by waterfalls
in the mountain lakes

for only a glimpse
the hike alone takes days

for the expanse
of mountains and their plains

can only be imagined
in the light of sun's rays

There rocks can fall
into grass and wild grains

perhaps hit a tree
that will bend its stained

bark and limbs to catch
the rolling wild plains

maybe bounce past a deer
or under an aeroplane

on a journey down a mountain
far from its moraine

creeks bubble silver
contrast the golden sway

but no matter who you ask
it's a magical place.

BLEEDING-HEART DOVE*

One day I hope to see
A bleeding-heart dove
One day one will fly
Soaring far above

For such a pretty creature
With such a fragile heart
Should never land on earth
Lest it be torn apart

One day I hope to feel
Those feathers crimson red
Across a chest of white
Where the bird has "bled"

For such a snowy blanket
Should never once be stained
And all dyes, wines, and blood
Should be wiped away with haste

One day I hope to find
Whoever fired the shot
Whoever loosed the arrow
That pierced my sweet bird's heart

For someone who'd harm
Something so innocent…
I could never fathom
someone so insolent

One day I hope to know
What kind of a god
Would paint something so sweet
To make art of a flaw

For such a vibrant colour
Such poetic beauty
The bird is born marred
Heart beating tragedy

One day I hope to ask
Through whistles, songs, and tweets
To ask the dove that always bleeds
How its heart still beats

For such an eternal wound
Must have a story
What world wouldn't give purpose
To a sight so sad and gory

One day I hope to see
A dove with a bleeding heart
One day I hope to see
The lovely tragic art

One day I hope to see
Sanctuary for the sanguinary
One day I hope to see
The crimson, scarlet, cherry

One day I hope to see
A bleeding-heart dove
And know despite its bleeding heart
If it can still feel love

Gallicolumba luzonica the "bleeding heart dove" is a "near-threatened species." See https://ebird.org/speciess/lubhea1 for pictures.

BETTER IN BLUE

Some people can stop
And enjoy the view
And some of us just happen
To look better in blue

I envy those persons
The natural optimists
Or those who live unaware
The true free populace

Who can choose to ignore
Those precious little things
Peeves and eyesores
Words, burns, stings

Those persons who can choose
To look on the bright side
Where yoga and breathing
Really clears their mind

And it's not that I'm sensitive
Or that I'm a pessimist
I just wish I could share
The positive sentiment

I appreciate my life
And the gifts that I notice
But to fix a problem
You have to focus

If somewhere in space
A creator exists
I think I was put here
To help and to fix

And if we be many
Or if we be few
Some of us humans
Look better in blue

We can try to wear yellow
Or other warm hues
But some of us will always
Look better in blue

ROSE*

Oh my Rose stained red
How is it, I wonder,
To live in your head
A porcelain Pearl
Contrasts with your world
Yet together you fit
Fast stead

For centuries you stayed
Side by side
But etiquette in love
Seemed not to abide
Who have you hurt with your sword?
Do we vilify the rose
'Cause it was born with thorns?
How many a time have we cried?

You Rose, pretty true
Prick the ingenue
For trying to pick you
Your reds and pinks
They drew us in
But I wonder what part
Is to blame for ruin.

Do we vilify the natural
For the harm it brings
Do we vilify the Siren
For the song it sings?
Do we blame the pearl
For the parasite inside
Do we blame the pearl
Since the mollusk must've died?

Rose oh Rose
Somewhere in those vines
Would I find
The bones of a creature
Some field mouse that died
That tried to scamper home
To beat the autumn chill
But got caught in the thrall
of your thorny bastille

This poem includes a vibe from Crystal Gems in Steven Universe.

SUNFLOWER

Have you ever seen a sunflower
Planted in a vase
And stuffed inside a kitchen
Reduced to a display

And do you know why sunflowers
All face the same direction
Identical in fields
A congregation, a collection

As if they've all turned
To face the eye of god
The thing that gives them life–
Do they deify the sun?

But stuffed inside a plant pot
Only windows give them life
But if they face the window
They cannot grace our eyes

So we turn them around
So we can see their yellow
Our little piece of sundrop
Our own personal meadow

It's no shock they wither
facing towards inside;
We try to bottle beauty
And deprive it of its life.

ROMANTICISE

(aka, I read Kuroshitsuji whilst recovering from emergency surgery)

Face flushed with fever
Cheeks glow ruby red
Egyptian cotton, sheets of satin
Opalescent bed

My voice rasps like a crow's
My head light as its feathers
Sweat soaks raven locks
To these quilts I'm tethered

And sleep does not escape me
Rather it takes flight
The world around me swirls
Impossibly light

As my cognition bends
Fevered dreams inspire
Give my mind time to wind
Because my body's tired

My skin is white as porcelain
Shimmering and pale
My limbs birdlike and delicate
Though you may call them frail

Why do I phrase it positively
When I'm in such decline
Because my coping strategy
Is to romanticise

Because to feel so poorly
Is really such a pain
It becomes priority
Just to keep myself sane:

Though it may be damaging
I ignore illness's hold;
Like ingenues of old
I find drama in a cold.

THE LITTLE THINGS*

First you'll notice it in the little things
Taking breaks while washing your hair
Opting for cream because the milk is too heavy
Counting your breaths on the stairs

First you'll notice it in the little things
Taking half a step at a time
Sitting in darkness cause you don't have
The strength to open the curtains
Cracking your knuckles after every
stanza is typed

First you'll notice it in the little things
Feeling nauseatingly empty
Feeling nothing but the lack

Circumstance forces your hand
To tell lies of omission
To pretend everything is fine
Despite worsening conditions

First you'll notice it in the little things
The ache that creeps its way up your body
Starting in your legs, settling in your spine
Ricocheting up and up
Shooting down your shoulders

In hindsight, all these things don't seem so little

*Joint hypermobility is caused by connective tissue disorders. Often referred to as "double-jointedness," hypermobility can be painful and damaging.

FEELING OF MINE

It's a constant companion
This feeling of mine
A relentless battle
To which I'm resigned

Sometimes it's far
Sometimes it's near
But always it's there
Whispering in my ear

My sleep is disturbed
By restless nights
Time is taken
By endless fights

Friendships weakened
By days occupied
My body is aching
This feeling of mine

DANDELIONS*

Delicate seems the dandelion
Seeds blown away by the wind
Fragile seems its petals
To be ripped, snatched, eaten
But I think we soon forget
What the dandelion endures
To swarm with yellow flowers

Yards and gardens overturned
Weed killer, grass
Deer, people, birds
The dandelions struggle through
Never being deterred

The flowers grow through concrete
Find homes in sidewalk cracks
You can pick them from the ground
Yet always they grow back

So go forth and hail
The flower so strong
Like us, who seemed weak
It was strongest all along.

This poem has been previously published in the North Carolina Bards Poetry Anthology.

Alastor George

CNN: THE WORLD'S ENDING (AGAIN)

My friends will drink and drive by the time they're 25
And their drunken drive-bys won't make the news
Like the one the day before or the fight on the dance floor
During prom night of twenty-twenty-two

And they'll do nine fingers a night by the time they're 9+5
And I reckon I'll be there in some ways too
If human Nature's to ignore what makes your eyes go sore
What's the point of keeping up the evening news?

Why report it every night when we're desensitised
Like the edible gummies that the kiddos chew?

Maybe the real core is less about the wars
Or whores outside the general stores
Or fights on the gymnasium floors
Or chores or gore or army corps
Or who we should or shouldn't deplore
Politicians with no rapport
The uncared-for or the liquor stores

The core is for us to care some more,
Because there are a few who   still   do.

And all of these, you'll find, by the time I'm 95
Will have found places or solutions to
Because some things are nature, before and evermore
But some things will pass, Like I and you.

www.ingramcontent.com/pod-product-compliance
Lightning Source LLC
Chambersburg PA
CBHW041725070526
44586CB00006B/78